WHEN
AN ANIMAL
GROWS

A Science I CAN READ Book

Harper & Row, Publishers · New York

WHEN
AN ANIMAL
GROWS

by Millicent E. Selsam

Pictures by John Kaufmann

For Stephanie Ellis

If Dr. George B. Schaller had not watched
the daily life of the Mountain Gorilla for almost two years
in the eastern Congo;

if Margaret M. Nice had not studied the life history
of the Song Sparrow for eight years;

if Dr. John Paul Scott and other scientists
had not observed the ways of sheep and the growth of lambs;

and if many observers of the Mallard Duck
had not recorded what they saw,

this book could not have been written.

This is the story of a baby gorilla.

He is very little and weak.

He is one day old.

And this is the story of a lamb

that grows up to be a sheep.

This lamb was born

just half an hour ago.

But already she can stand up

on her wobbly legs.

The baby gorilla will grow.

And the lamb will grow.

But they will grow in different ways.

Some animals grow slowly,

like the gorilla that is helpless at first

And some grow fast, like the lamb.

Birds grow in different ways too.

When a sparrow comes from an egg,

it can't see and has no feathers.

But a duck walks and swims

after its mother, soon after hatching.

Either way, an animal grows.

It gets bigger and bigger.

And before long it is grown-up

and able to take care of itself.

The baby gorilla's mother

has milk to nurse her baby.

She holds him tight.

At night the baby gorilla

sleeps with his mother

in a nest of branches.

He is with her all the time.

The mother sheep has milk

for her baby too.

Soon the lamb finds the right spot.

She fills her stomach with warm milk.

This makes her sleepy.

The lamb nurses and sleeps,

and nurses and sleeps.

Mother and baby gorilla are not alone.

They live with other gorillas in the forest

The band of gorillas is resting.

They have just eaten

a lot of leaves, stems, and roots.

They are ready to move on

to a new place.

The big, old gorilla

with silver hair on his back

gives the signal. He is the leader.

The mother gorilla

picks up her baby in one arm

and carries him close to her chest.

Now she walks on two legs and one arm.

The mother sheep is not alone either.

She lives with many other mother sheep

and their lambs in a flock.

The baby lamb

follows her mother.

She runs along at her side.

She starts to nibble

at the grass.

The oldest mother sheep in the flock

gives a signal when it is time to move.

She is the leader.

The mother sheep follows the others.

The baby lamb follows her.

The baby gorilla grows and grows.

Now he is three months old.

Now when his mother

puts him on the ground,

he can crawl away.

But not too far.

If he does, the mother gorilla

pulls him back to her side.

The baby lamb is only a few weeks old.

When she goes too far away,

the mother sheep calls "Baaaaa."

And the baby lamb runs to her side.

If the baby lamb gets lost,

she calls "Baaaaaa."

The mother sheep hears her cry

and goes to find her.

The three-month-old baby gorilla

starts to ride on his mother's back.

As he rides he slaps the leaves.

Sometimes he grabs a bit of a plant

and stuffs it into his mouth.

He has teeth now.

He can eat leaves and stems.

The little lamb nurses less and less
and eats more and more grass.

The baby gorilla keeps growing.

He is six months old now.

He is still getting milk from his mother,

but he is eating more and more plants.

Already he can climb by himself.

He can walk behind his mother.

He can swing sideways

and upside down.

Now the baby gorilla is a year old.

When his mother rests,

he plays with other baby gorillas.

Four of them are playing a game.

It looks like follow-the-leader

that children play.

The leader runs along a branch.

The others follow.

The leader climbs up a vine.

The others follow.

The leader slides down.

The others slide down too.

The leader holds on to a vine

and stretches way out.

Snap! The vine breaks.

The leader falls.

And down after him

come his friends,

vine leaves and all.

They tumble softly

into the leaves below.

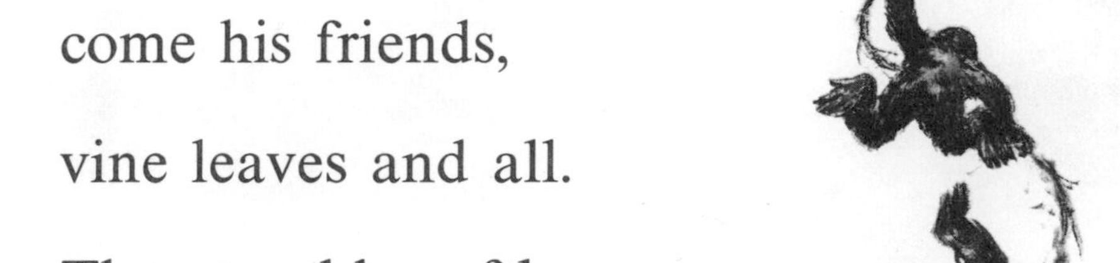

The baby lamb plays with other lambs

when she is only a few weeks old.

Lambs play follow-the-leader too.

They run after each other

through the green fields.

They jump on the rock.

They jump off the rock.

If one jumps up

and turns around in the air,

the others jump up and turn around

in the air.

Baby gorillas play another game.

It is like our "king of the mountain."

One baby gorilla sits on a stump.

The others try to push him off.

Bang! He gives them a kick.

He is still king of the mountain.

He stays there until

another baby gorilla pushes him off.

Then there is a new king.

Lambs play king of the mountain too.

Baby gorillas wrestle.

Here one of them has a headlock
on another one.

Here is a fight between two baby lambs.

They are facing each other.

Their heads are low. They charge!

Crack! Their heads bang together.

Then they move away.

Then they do it again.

It's just a game!

Sometimes baby gorillas

play by themselves.

The leaves are their toys.

Here is a baby gorilla

with a big bunch of leaves in his hand.

He bangs them on the ground.

He swings them over his head.

Sometimes he tears the leaves

with his hands

and lets them slowly fall around him

in a green shower.

Sometimes he puts the leaves upside down

on his head

and just sits under his hat.

But baby lambs always play together.

Every once in a while the baby gorilla

goes to sit near his mother.

The baby lamb goes to her mother too,

every once in a while.

She lies down next to her

in the shade of a big tree.

When the mother gorilla

moves through the forest,

the baby gorilla still rides on her back

or he may walk behind her.

When the mother sheep gets on her feet

and starts to walk away,

the little lamb gets up too

and follows her mother.

The baby gorilla

gets less and less milk from his mother.

By the time he is a year and a half old,

he eats only stems, roots, and leaves.

But he still stays close to his mother

when he is not playing.

The little lamb nurses

only for a few months.

Then she eats only grass.

She is grown-up.

When she is a year old, she can

have a little lamb of her own.

But the baby gorilla is still growing.

He grows and grows.

He stays with his mother

until he is three years old.

Now he makes his own nest

to sleep in at night.

His mother has had another baby.

The new baby is small and weak.

It needs its mother.

But the young gorilla

is big enough now

to take care of himself.

He takes his place in the gorilla band.

Birds, like other animals, grow too.

These are sparrow's eggs.

These are duck's eggs.

The baby sparrows

grow inside the eggs for twelve days.

Now they are pecking at their shells.

They will soon be out.

Here is one. Here is another.

Here is sparrow number three.

And here is number four.

They are Song Sparrows.

The baby ducks

grow inside the eggs for almost a month.

Then they begin to peck

at their shells.

Now a wet little duckling comes out.

Now another comes out.

And another. And another.

And another and another

and another and another.

They are Mallard ducklings.

The little sparrows are in a nest

hidden in the grass.

They are tiny and helpless.

They have no feathers.

They can't see. They can't walk.

How different the ducklings are.

They have soft little feathers.

They can see.

As soon as the ducklings are dry,

the mother duck clucks quietly.

She leaves the nest.

The little ducks follow.

The mother duck walks into the water.

She swims.

The ducklings waddle into the water.

They swim too.

Here comes the mother sparrow with food.

Up go four heads. Four mouths open.

The baby sparrow

with his head the highest

and his beak open the widest gets fed.

The mother sparrow flies away.

She comes back with more food.

Now another baby sparrow gets the food.

Father sparrow brings food too.

Both parents are busy all day long

catching insects

to take back to the nest.

When it is cold,

or if the sun is too hot,

mother sparrow spreads her wings

over the little sparrows.

The ducklings do not have to be fed.

They find their own food on the water.

They eat any bugs, beetles, or flies

on top of the water.

The mother duck tips down

into the water

and eats the plants and seeds

she finds there.

At night the mother duck

leads her ducklings to the shore.

She spreads her wings over them

and keeps them warm.

The father duck goes off by himself.

The mother duck

takes care of the ducklings.

The little sparrows grow bigger.

Here they are three days old.

Their feathers are starting to grow.

Their eyes are beginning to open.

The mother and father sparrow

keep bringing food.

The little sparrows grow and grow.

Six days old.

The sparrows can stand up now.

Their feathers are growing

longer and longer.

Their eyes are wide open.

Eight days old.

The sparrows are well covered

with feathers.

They move around in the nest.

They even climb to the edge.

Ten days old.

The sparrows are about to hop

out of the nest.

Here goes one.

And another.

And the next.

And the last.

They are all gone.

The sparrows do not

go too far.

They move around in the bushes

near the nest.

During the next few days

they start to fly.

Each little sparrow is alone.

But each one can hear

the mother and father sparrow.

And the mother and father sparrow

can hear them.

When they call "Eep!" their parents

can find them in the bushes

and give them food.

If danger is near, the mother or father

sparrow calls "Tik, tik, tik,"

and the young sparrows keep very quiet.

Then they are hard to find.

But where do the ducklings hide

when there is danger?

Here comes a turtle.

The mother duck cries out.

The ducklings clump together behind her.

But now the turtle is too close.

The mother duck quacks loudly.

The ducklings hide in the water plants.

The mother duck flaps her wings.

The turtle follows, but she keeps ahead.

When they are far from the ducklings,

the mother duck flies up into the air.

She goes back and calls her ducklings.

They come to her. They are safe now.

The sparrows stay in the bushes

around the nest

until they are seventeen days old.

Then they come out of hiding.

The four baby sparrows

find each other again.

They can fly well now.

The sparrows are twenty-one days old.

They still follow their parents

for food, even though

they can find their own food now.

When father sparrow sings,

they pop up beside him.

Sometimes they land on top of him!

At one month the sparrows are grown-up.

They feed themselves.

They fly around.

They call "Tsip, tsip" to each other.

The ducklings take longer to grow up.

All through the warm days of summer

they swim, eat, and rest.

It is two months before they have

all the feathers they need to fly.

Here is one young duck

scooting across the water.

His wings are flapping.

Another week or so

and the whole family of ducklings

is flying.

The duck family is grown-up now.

The young ducks join other ducks.

And one day in the fall,

flock after flock takes to the air

and flies south.

The young sparrows fly south

in the fall too.

Next year

the birds will fly back north.

The sparrows and ducks

that were babies the year before

will raise their own families.